CHARLES FAUDREE
Details

CHARLES FAUDREE
Details

CHARLES FAUDREE *with* FRANCESANNE TUCKER

Photography by JENIFER JORDAN

GIBBS SMITH
TO ENRICH AND INSPIRE HUMANKIND

First Edition
15 14 13 12 11   5 4 3 2 1

Text © 2011 by Charles Faudree
Photographs © 2011 by Jenifer Jordan

Published by
Gibbs Smith
P.O. Box 667
Layton, Utah 84041

1.800.835.4993 orders
www.gibbs-smith.com

Designed by Rita Sowins / Sowins Design
Printed and bound in China
Gibbs Smith books are printed on either recycled, 100% post-consumer waste, FSC-certified papers
or on paper produced from sustainable PEFC-certified forest/controlled wood source. Learn more at
www.pefc.org.

Library of Congress Cataloging-in-Publication Data

Faudree, Charles.
  Charles Faudree details / Charles Faudree with Francesanne Tucker ; photography by Jenifer Jordan.
— 1st ed.
    p. cm.
  ISBN 978-1-4236-1174-5
  1. Faudree, Charles—Themes, motives. 2. Interior decoration—United States. I. Tucker,
Francesanne. II. Jordan, Jenifer. III. Title.
  NK2004.3.F38A4 2011
  747.092—dc22
                        2011013850

Previous overleaf: A sampling of prized pieces from one of my collections highlights my desktop tablescape. Included are antique watch holders and, inevitably, representatives of my ever-growing parade of cherished dog figures. *Right:* A painted entry lantern and a pair of lamps illuminate a soaring entry hall.

I dedicate this book to those who inspire me.

CONTENTS

I *have waited a long time to write this book; I guess*
I've been a little reluctant to come to the end of a project I've dreamed about for
so many years. Details may seem like a small subject, but these finishing accessories are by far the most important part of decorating. People's lives are expressed
by little details. They give a room its soul.

Too often people go to a lot of trouble to create a perfect room and stop just
before they've made it truly theirs. These final steps can include everything from
arranging a wonderful tabletop, creating wallscapes, and adding the interest
of books, to the smallest touches, such as locating the right scented candle or
choosing the perfect fringe for a pillow. Details are like the frosting on the cake,
and who doesn't like frosting best?

Examining the way people dress is an excellent place to study the effect of
details. People express who they are and what they like by the things they wear.
Bold necklaces show a bold spirit. Cowboy boots and big silver buckles say it
all. My sister Francie's ever curious, outgoing personality shines through her
unusual and wonderful glasses. Despite the limitations of jackets and slacks, I
can express my love of fabric with my pocket handkerchiefs and bow ties.

In the same way, the details of a room create its identity. The accessories we
display, their color and texture, abundance or restraint, similarity or variety,
combine to establish a unique personality for each room. The way we put them
together is art. It's what it's all about.

Some of my favorite rooms are densely layered. Silks with linens, checks with
stripes, and florals with toiles—in the right hands—can be used in wonderful
combinations in a single room. Objects from different countries and centuries
add more layers of interest. I have been a standard bearer for all things French for
much of my life, but when you cross borders and add English, Asian and Swed-
ish influences, punctuated with contemporary pieces, you only enrich the mix.

Adding detail is the point where creating a special one-of-a-kind room hap-
pens. Every room can have its own mood, personality and charm. It's up to us to
create it. In *Details,* I'll show you not just the results but the wonderful journey
that is part of the process.

TABLESCAPES

When you are lucky enough to find the perfect table for a room, you're just getting started. Whether it is a flawless antique or a spectacular contemporary piece, a table is, after all, meant to hold things. No matter how beautiful, a table looks lost with nothing on it. A tablescape—an artistic composition of accessories—provides the essential finishing detail.

At its best, a tablescape can be more than a grouping of artfully placed objects adorning a lovely piece of furniture. It presents an opportunity to include memories of friends and adventures to be enjoyed on a daily basis.

I have a wonderful tortoiseshell box that is not only a prominent piece in my tablescape but also a reminder of the cherished friend who gave it to me. An unforgettable outing to the Paris flea market comes to mind every time I see the bronze lamps that are indispensable to the buffet they highlight. And my antique French coal-burning stove is a spectacular jardinière (meaning "cache pot") accessory as well as a warm reminder of a special client.

* * *

I encourage people to keep the objects they love out in the open, where everyone can see and enjoy them. But taking advantage of the treasures you accumulate over the years becomes skillful decorating only if you combine them effectively.

While it is important to arrange a tablescape with care and a critical eye, there is no particular formula. As a rough guide, the mass or weight of one or more objects on one side of the grouping should be balanced equally on the other side. That leaves only what is the most difficult part: deciding which accessories to include.

The best way to decide what goes together and what doesn't is to experiment. Try a group of favorite objects together. Take something away; try something else in its place. Trust your eye. Successful tablescapes add depth and interest to the furniture they embellish. Creating a pleasing tablescape can add as much to a room as a good piece of art.

Finally, don't forget flowers as a finishing touch to your tablescape. Flowers mix with everything and frequently they add a delicate fragrance to their surroundings. Whether it is a single blossom or an impressive centerpiece, the addition of flowers to a table makes everything else come alive.

Opening overleaf: Rare tortoiseshell boxes that I have collected for more than forty years form the backbone of an outstanding tablescape. *Previous page:* My first collection, antique English Battersea boxes, is assembled into an impressive tablescape on an antique silver tray. *Above:* Establishing a relationship between unlike objects adds to the interest of a tablescape. An antique French figurine is a three-dimensional companion to the painted figures on the English foot tub.

Above: The smallest detail can have an outsized impact. This handsome Minton Spidell painted chest gets a decorative boost from its beautifully tasseled key. *Opposite:* My affection for dogs adds charm and continuity to this tablescape in my guest bedroom, a dog lover's retreat. An antique tole lamp illuminates figurines from my extensive canine collection. A wallscape above continues the theme with an antique terra-cotta dog's head and an oil painting of resting hounds.

Any one of these tortoiseshell boxes would be an important accessory. Displayed together, the collection is a remarkable tablescape. Two antique blackamoor bud vases stand at the periphery.

Opposite: The sophistication of crystal lamps, silver frames and orchids is a pleasing contrast to the antique French farm table in Susie Collins' entry hall. *Right:* Linear placement unifies interesting accessories on David and Cindy Foster's coffee table.

"Nothing adds more to the warmth and personality of a room than objects and photographs of ones you love."

Above: Fresh roses from the garden, antique transferware and a Black Forest wooden castle box create a charming tablescape for Bob and Penny Downing's breakfast table.

Opposite: A blue-and-white cachepot, platter and tureen are illuminated by a custom Staffordshire lamp in this appealing tablescape composition in Drew and Ginny Webb's home.

Above: The doleful gaze of the hounds in this painting, *The Uninvited Guest,* directs the eye to an appealing tablescape atop a painted chest in my cabin. *Opposite:* For a tablescape at my cabin, custom salt glaze pottery lamps and wooden candlesticks are used to flank a wonderful Mettlach urn with a Paris flea market past.

Opposite: A Staffordshire figure of Giuseppe Garibaldi, a nineteenth-century Italian military hero, forms the base of a custom lamp that illuminates a tablescape in my library. Additional Staffordshire figures add interest to the library shelves beyond. *Above:* Stacked books offer height and a platform for wonderful small accessories, including a Black Forest clock holder. A small bouquet adds to the color introduced by papier mâché trays.

Above: A fur clutch on a stack of books creates a scene that hints at a gala night ahead. Small tablescapes such as this one add interesting detail just about anywhere, including this unexpected location on top of an antique painted Italian chair that graces Roger and Kelly Ganner's master bathroom. *Opposite:* A pewter tureen and chalice balance a tall pewter candlestick lamp on top of an intricately carved tribal table in Larry and Carol Bump's home.

Opposite: Traditional accessories, including a Rose Medallion covered dish, contrast with the contemporary edge of a custom game table. The French chair is from Dennis and Leen.

Above: A faux bois cup of fresh flowers breathes life into a small tablescape.

A bronze dog collection on a rare upholstery-topped table is upstaged by the real thing, my much-photographed Cavalier King Charles spaniel Nicholas.

"If you fall in love
        with something,
    that's all that matters."

Opposite: A bust and a pair of antique wooden urns converted into lamps create a refined tablescape for an eighteenth-century Provençal commode that serves as a focal point in Roger and Kelly Ganner's living room. A prominent gilded mirror completes the classic elegance of the setting. *Above:* Details can play an important role in uniting different elements in a room. The fabric trim on the lampshade repeats the pillow fabric, creating a pleasing link between the tablescape and the adjoining sofa. Using crystal for several different objects in the tablescape composition reinforces their relationship.

Above: A variety of textures adds interest to a tablescape in Mark and Cassie Shires' home. Majolica, tortoiseshell, rattan and fresh hydrangeas contribute. *Opposite:* A spectacular Italian chest holds an international tablescape in my new home. Custom lamps made from Oriental vases flank an English foot tub and an antique French figurine. A French trumeau mirror hangs above.

Above left: With thoughtful selection and arrangement, utilitarian bath accessories double as an attractive tablescape. Antique and new silver pieces include a soap dish that repeats the carving in the sink stand. *Above right:* Commonplace mouthwash becomes a colorful ornament when stored in an old chemist's bottle. This tablescape in my bath also benefits from an antique Guerlain cologne bottle and a single white lily in a silver bud vase. *Opposite:* A tablescape of silver accessories frames an impressionistic painting that is, in reality, a reflection of the carefully placed art on the wall opposite this dressing table.

WALL
DECORATIONS

The things we choose to hang on our walls should have a special significance, because they are the details that set the tone for an entire room. Frequently our prominent wall decorations are paintings, and I have always thought the true value of a painting, or any other artwork, has less to do with its pedigree than the emotional response it creates in us. Its beauty comes from our feelings for it, not from the signature at the bottom.

My choices are largely curiosities rather than great art. I have a portrait of a Scottish child that has been a centerpiece of my wall decorations as I've moved from home to home over the years. It has no Rembrandt pretensions, but it is dear to me and I wouldn't dream of parting with it.

Collecting this kind of highly personal art is a lifelong process. It's a much greater challenge—and adventure—to find art on your own than to go through a broker. I recommend buying only paintings that you love. If you find a work by an unknown artist that later appreciates in value, you've gotten a happy investment bonus in addition to the pleasure the piece of art has given you.

Regardless of monetary value, one special painting may take center stage if, for instance, you choose to showcase it above a mantel. In other cases, it's nice to combine a number of paintings into a larger wallscape—a complementary grouping of wall decorations. As is true of tablescapes, a wallscape's success depends on what is pleasing to the eye.

I like to include more than one element in a wallscape. For example, including prints and engravings with paintings adds interest. Incorporating a wall bracket or sconce with a group of paintings and prints adds a whole new dimension. It illustrates the philosophy I've expressed in all of my previous books: "It's all about the mix, not the match."

Using pairs is one of the easiest ways to introduce more elements into an effective wallscape. As long as you are mindful of scale, it's hard to go wrong with a pair of candelabra flanking a mirror. You can achieve the same result with brackets on either side of a painting. China collections are a wonderful source for wallscapes. Plates in different sizes can be used to surround a large platter, painting, or mirror. If you are fortunate enough to have heirloom china, it will bring a sense of history to the display.

Wallscapes are important, but they are not the only effective display for art. Sometimes the best place to hang a prized painting is the unexpected one. I love to see little pictures hanging on bookcase dividers, or standing on shelves alongside the books. A small painting propped against another object adds charm to a tablescape or a mantel. A small wallscape, tucked beneath the stairs, is equally unexpected and delightful. If you really love a painting, or any piece of art, you will find a place for it.

Opening overleaf: Continuity in a small wallscape can amplify its impact. An antique oil painting of a hound is reinforced by a pair of bronze canines resting on tole brackets. *Previous page:* An oval horn mirror emphasizes the rustic nature of the painted stone wall and country French commode in the Fore home. A coral print fabric shade on the English gin barrel custom lamp adds a splash of color. *Above:* An antique oil painting of an adorable terrier on the planked wall of my cabin is a solo wall decoration, but it is enhanced by a large supporting cast of canines. The worn and wonderful metal chair below holds an antique dog figure and three volumes in praise of dogs.

The pastoral feel of a blue-and-white porcelain-filled cupboard wallscape is reinforced by the fabulous Mettlach German tureen centerpiece on the table. The chandelier features real candles.

Opposite: Serenity was important in the selection of decorations for the Theta sorority at the University of Oklahoma. Above a French commode, I flanked a painting with simple pairs of urns, lamps and figurines. Fabric for the wing chairs is "Biron Check" from The Charles Faudree Collection for Vervain. *Above:* The heavy usage of the entry hall of the Kappa Alpha Theta house at the University of Oklahoma dictates a gracious but unfussy treatment. A crystal lamp, three blue-and-white pieces and fresh greenery, reflected in a beautiful mirror, are all the featured chest needs to look elegant.

Right: A handsome antique French clock is a freestanding wallscape that has been a decorative traveling companion with me to many of my homes. *Opposite:* A large, unadorned dog portrait is a suitably restrained wallscape for a sleek contemporary fireplace wall in Larry and Carol Bump's home. The accompanying painted wall sconces blend perfectly with the travertine surface.

"One of life's greatest pleasures is living with paintings you love."

A single painting of utmost simplicity can dominate a room, as demonstrated by the large garden panel from the Bunny Williams Collection in David and Cindy Foster's den.

Above: Every component of this corner of the Fore den contributes to its easy country atmosphere, from the English candlestick lamps and a bronze rooster, to the French country sideboard and chairs, to the small detail of a topiary rosemary plant. But it is the layering of antique oil paintings, with one propped against another, that adds particular charm to the setting. *Opposite:* A landing in Frank and Gayle Eby's home is the perfect perch for a wall-scape of antique bird's-nest prints. A fanciful bird pillow and a daybed in pastel egg colors amplify the theme.

Opposite: The corner of the Shires' living room is filled with a table and comfortable antique French chairs. Adding to the warmth is an oil painting of a lamb and Black Forest accessories.

Above: A Paris flea market find of a Black Forest gun rack is used to display Mark's collection of antique canes.

Above left: A sizable wallscape composed of Jimmy Steinmeyer watercolor renderings transforms a blank staircase wall into an art showcase. *Above right:* Stairways require extensive wall space that cries out for a pretty wallscape. Here, a French swag clock anchors an artfully arranged collection of antique landscapes. *Opposite:* Wallscapes and tablescapes frequently work together to create a single pleasing display. A pair of antique French prints is flanked by a pair of brackets to form the wallscape, but they also are flanked by urns holding tole leaves that are a feature of the accompanying tablescape.

Opposite: A French bibliothèque accentuates the height of the Ganners' living room and showcases Chinese export porcelain. *Above:* A floor-to-ceiling wallscape is produced by a French cupboard that draws the eye to the end of a hallway in Roger and Kelly Ganner's home. Collections of porcelains and books stand out against red painted shelves. Attention to detail is evident in the repletion of the shelf color in the collections.

Above: Diversity adds special appeal to a wallscape in Tom and Mickey Harris's cabin. A sea bird and stone pigeon share space above a Mexican *santos,* an orchid in a wooden bowl and a small lead box. *Opposite:* A wallscape over a French commode in Drew and Ginny Webb's home is composed of a symmetrical arrangement of pairs. Bracketed blue-and-white plates are separated by a stacked pair of antique maps. A pair of red tole lamps and blue-and-white cachepots continue the symmetry on the tablescape below.

Opposite: Matched pairs of blue-and-white English china flank an antique Federal bull's-eye mirror with spread-winged eagle cartouche. An elaborate tassel hanging from the eagle's beak adds a touch of whimsy to the wallscape. *Above left:* A celadon jar on a glided eagle bracket forms the centerpiece for a collection of antique plates and trays from my collection. *Above right:* Not all culinary masterpieces start in the oven. In my kitchen, a lovely old bracket adds three-dimensional interest to a blue-and-white china still life. Antique food pots continue the display on the countertop.

Above: An elaborate gilded English mirror and plates from Kelly Ganner's collection of English stoneware are combined to form a wallscape in the dining room. Serving pieces from the collection adorn the 18th-century Italian commode beneath the wallscape.

Opposite: A wonderful collection of green majolica complements the antique Black Forest mirror on the Ebys' landing.

Opposite: Lined with checked fabric, a French cupboard offers a perfect country backdrop for a wallscape display of red-and-white transferware and antique Staffordshire cows and chickens in Jeffrey and Lisa Rowsey's home. *Right:* A marvelous collection of blue-and-white export porcelain creates this wallscape in a painted cupboard in my dining room. The finishing natural cotton tassel is an antique.

Above: With attention to detail, the desirable qualities of modern fixtures and antiques can both be enjoyed. Here, a contemporary television framed by an antique plate rack easily blends into a traditional wallscape. *Opposite:* An extensive wallscape creates a perfect spot for tea in a cozy corner of Bob and Penny Downing's breakfast room. A large number of the collection's antique W. Smith and Company transferware pieces were an anniversary gift from Bob.

Opposite: The simplicity of an open display of everyday white china creates an effective and useful wallscape in David and Cindy Foster's kitchen. *Above:* A trompe l'oeil cluster of hanging garlic is a subtle yet delightful adornment for a cupboard in my kitchen.

Above: A cotton tassel adds just the right touch of ornamentation to an old painted chest. *Opposite:* Layering patterns adds depth to this wallscape, where wreath-patterned wallpaper forms the background for antique botanical prints. Fabric on the dining room chairs repeats the wallpaper's design.

Opposite: The imposing size of the chinoiserie sideboard in Frank and Leigh Ann Fore's home needs only a single contemporary watercolor of impressive dimension for balance. Below, greenery in a pewter tankard adds a living repetition of the impression of foliage in the artwork. *Right:* Antique books and aquatic accessories in muted colors create a quiet wall-scape. A French chair and pillow in watery blue fabrics complete the setting.

Opposite: The theme for the bunk room at the Shires' country home is apparent with the Currier & Ives framed dog prints and the hunting dog wallpaper. *Above:* The bunk room is pleasingly decorated with a mix of stripes, checks and toile wallpaper all in chocolate brown.

"Only your eye can tell you what you will be happy with."

Left: An antique French clock painted by Janet Fadler Davie pulls the eye to the end of the upstairs hall of the Eby home. *Opposite:* A collection of framed butterflies celebrates the beauty of nature in this wallscape in the Harris cabin guest room.

Opposite: The original bath is enhanced with a collection of colored owl engravings, while a stone pigeon adds a little humor to the room. *Above:* Medallions on the wallpaper inspire this wallscape, which includes medallion-monogrammed towels and bird's-nest prints.

Above: A grouping of framed botanicals, antique French mirror and a pair of gilded brackets holding celadon vases adds much dimension to the bedroom wall at the Shires' home.

Opposite: A collection of antique fabric can be framed to form a striking wallscape. Aubusson tapestries that once covered chair pillows now flank a French mirror in an elegant display over a painted French chest in the Ganners' master bathroom.

MANTELS

There's a very good reason for the old greeting "Pull a chair up to the fire." The cheerfulness and comfort we associate with a fireplace make it a logical gathering place. It is the focal point of any room and the first place that draws our eye. Consequently, the details we use to accessorize the fireplace surround and mantel should be most carefully selected.

Fireplaces make a strong decorative statement even before they are embellished. Old carved wooden mantels, sleek streamlined hearths, and elegant marble fireplaces all have distinct personalities. Their decorations should magnify and reinforce the welcoming ambiance of these areas.

Even if a contemporary fireplace surround has no mantel; I still like to hang something on it when possible. An antique French barometer or an old painting, for example, provides interesting contrast as well as calling attention to the fireplace itself.

More frequently, a mantel is present. I like the idea of a graceful pair of candelabra here, with perhaps a treasured mirror hanging above. The addition of fresh flowers is particularly charming

* * *

because it is unexpected and shows hospitality by this thoughtful attention to detail.

The mantel over my living room fireplace holds a pair of Chinese export jars, a pair of candlesticks, and a French ormolu clock I purchased on my very first trip to England. Above it is an impressionistic painting of a chair that has played different roles in my homes for many years.

I love mirrors over mantels, particularly when there is something wonderful to reflect. The mirror above my bedroom mantel reflects a painting that adds a touch of humor, as well as beauty, to its surroundings. It is a portrait of my instant ancestor, "Uncle Albert," a favorite relative I purchased over forty years ago.

The space beneath a mantel deserves attention too. In summer, a fireplace benefits from a little extra detail to avoid the appearance of a cold firebox. A needlepoint fireplace screen is a typical disguise for traditional fireplace hearths. I also like to arrange magnolia leaves here. Beautifully stacked birch logs are another attractive option.

Opening overleaf: Many of my favorite accessories come from buying expeditions to Europe. The ornate ormolu clock with rider is one of those treasures, found in Bath on my first trip to England. From its central location on my living room mantel, the lovely old piece contributes both elegance and fond memories. *Previous page:* Two unusual and lovely accessory pairs—bronze candelabra and carved gilt vases—add interest to the ormolu clock centerpiece atop an antique French fireplace mantel in my bedroom. A handsome French antique mirror gets an extra boost from its reflected image, a painting of my instant ancestor, "Uncle Albert." *Above:* The French stone mantel is adorned with an antique gilded French barometer and tole bouquets.

Restrained accessories for the limestone fireplace make a major contribution to their setting. A pair of lamps radiates charm. And both the greenery in the central tole vase and the fern adding freshness to the summer firebox echo the antique botanicals hanging above.

Opposite: A limestone fireplace mantel features Staffordshire pieces and tole containers whose vertical bouquets draw the eye toward the lofty over mantel in Jeffrey and Lisa Rowsey's home. *Above:* Classic accessories reinforce the beauty of an English carved and painted wood fireplace in John and Terry Mabrey's home. A pair of silver peacocks and a silver urn have a smaller scale that accommodates the placement of the oil painting above them. French painted and gilded wooden urns grace the mantel corners.

Above: Subdued tones dominate mantel decorations at the Theta sorority at the University of Oklahoma. A gold-toned painting is flanked by antique candelabra and a small pair of lions. Facing the mantel, blue porcelain and hydrangeas, accompanied by a pair of French candlesticks, comprise a simple tablescape. *Opposite:* An antique Regency marble fireplace in my living room displays some of my favorite belongings. A pair of blue-and-white export porcelain vases and a pair of candlesticks of kneeling blackamoor figures flank a lovely ormolu clock. Above, an impressionistic still life painting is a much-loved possession that has hung in many of my homes as well as in my sister's home, and has even served occasional decorating stints in the homes of friends.

Opposite: Accessories that reflect a personal interest add charm to interior design. Here, the decoration of the library mantel with bronze spaniel dog figurines celebrates the Bashaw family's favorite breed. The spaniel painting that is the mantel's focal point continues the theme. *Right:* A cast limestone mantel by Jim Kelly holds a pair of tole containers that pick up the dominant color in Jeffrey and Lisa Rowsey's den. Lighted black-amoor hurricane lamps and a fire in the firebox add a cheerful welcome to the setting.

"The details of decorating give a home its soul."

Above: Shades of a single color can create a beautiful setting. The mantel in Jeff and Sheryl Bashaw's home is filled with blue-and-white vases surrounding a wonderful old Imari plate. Upholstered pieces also are in shades of blue, and the French painting above the mantel is punctuated with a blue-roofed cottage. *Opposite:* A fireplace that was an original part of Steve and Gayle Allen's home has been antiqued and whitewashed to create a quiet background for accessories. Lighted ram's horn candlesticks and brass urns filled with moss balls bracket an interesting contemporary mirror with antiqued glass. Stacked birch logs fill the firebox.

Opposite: A single pair of painted stone baskets makes an understated but effective accessory. The old timber used for the mantel supports the rustic setting. *Above:* The bedroom mantel in my country home displays a cornucopia of woodsy delights. Stone urns constrain, with artless perfection, an overflowing arrangement of twigs and antlers. A pair of horn containers and a bronze deer sculpture complete the scene.

Above left: The outdoor room at Mark and Cassie Shires' cabin has perfect mantel shelf accompaniments: a folk art wooden cabin birdhouse and a stone pigeon. A rustic wrought-iron candelabrum completes the composition. *Above right:* An antique painting of a battle scene on Drew and Ginny Webb's mantel shelf anchors a traditional mantel treatment, including pairs of vases and Delft cows. Photographer Jenifer Jordan's rescue puppy, Parker, takes a break on an ottoman covered with "Biron Check" fabric from The Charles Faudree Collection for Vervain. *Opposite:* A painting propped on a timber shelf separates pewter containers and pewter candleholders, which are apt accessories for the mellow native stone fireplace in Mark and Cassie Shires' country home. The solemn gaze of the hounds in the painting rests on one of a pair of wing chairs covered in a fabric from The Charles Faudree Collection for Vervain.

Opposite: A wall of old French paneling, or *boiserie,* from a French chateau, has been transplanted to the Harris's Oklahoma "cabin." Blossom, the family's papillon dog, is nearly as exotic as her perch, an iron frame dressmaker's chair covered with faux bois fabric.

Above: The French mantel features a shell cross and roses in a memory teapot decorated with bits of glass.

Above: An antique English carved wooden fireplace contributes its own adornment to the two pairs of vases on its mantel. The majolica bird vases repeat the avian theme established by a pair of antique musical birdcages on a nearby French table. *Opposite:* Natural colors and textures highlight this commanding limestone fireplace. Stately tole floral branches in iron urns and a pair of rock crystal obelisks emphasize the height of the fireplace. A formal fireplace screen covers the firebox, while stone fruit baskets embellish the hearth.

Opposite: Sheaves of greenery in tole containers and a lush floral oil painting enliven an august antique limestone Regency fireplace in John and Terry Mabrey's home. The antique metal tureen on the mantel might well have graced a long-ago garden luncheon in such a setting. *Above:* A romantic mantel treatment in Bob and Penny Downing's living room includes exotic porcelains holding stargazer lilies and antique majolica parrots flanking a painting, *Intermission,* by Alan Maley.

FABRICS

For years I toyed with the idea of starting a furniture line, but when two companies in the same month asked me to do a fabric line; I took it as a sign and created The Charles Faudree Collection for Vervain. I know fabrics and I love them. From the first day, designing the line has been a deeply rewarding experience.

The inspiration for my first fabric design lay, literally, at my feet. "Cavalier," my cornerstone fabric, is a toile that includes my two Cavalier spaniels discreetly tucked into the design. It is an original toile that will be documented. I can't decorate without checks or stripes, which dictated more designs. Also, every room needs a little animal print, so they were included. Now I am adding to my fabric line and starting a trim line.

Fabric details are just as important as furniture. You can buy fabulous antiques, but without the magic of the right fabrics to complement them, you've compromised their impact. Fabrics introduce color, pattern and texture. To take full advantage of fabrics, I like to use a solid-colored sofa as a neutral canvas for pillows in several

*** ✳ ✳ ✳

different fabrics. Pillows are a wonderfully effective way to introduce more fabrics. Curtains are equally useful.

I love to use three, or even four, toiles in a room. Or checks in two different sizes. You can easily include seven or eight fabrics in a room, as long as they are compatible. The secret is, as always, in the mix—of pattern and texture—of prints, checks and toiles; of silks, linens and velvets. You can use them all. But carefully. You don't want to get so carried away that you wind up with a chair that looks as if it could pop corn. Unfortunately, there is no formula for mixing fabrics; it's simply magic.

More often than not, I start a room with one pivotal fabric. In the long run, it may not be the most important fabric—it may even wind up in the kitchen—but it starts the process. If your process starts with a pivotal fabric that is shockingly expensive, please do not abandon it. A pivotal fabric that is used sparingly on pillows or lampshades can still set the direction for a wonderful room.

My current home is subtle. But quiet as it is, I added one chintz for a little punch. I consider it to be my pivotal fabric. Chintz is wonderful. I think I read that Billy Baldwin once said when you've lived long enough to see chintz come back into style three times, you've lived too long. This humorous statement makes a good point: fabric styles are cyclical. Chintz is making a comeback in my house now. And I suspect there's going to be even more chintz in my future.

Opening overleaf: Plain headboard fabric is a foil for decorative pillows in a bedroom at Mark and Cassie Shires' home. A touch of leopard print calls attention to a French child's chair that, with the simple addition of a riser, has been transformed into stylish pet steps for the family dog. *Previous page:* In the right hands, more than one print can be used to add charm to a room. "Beauclaire" fabric used on an armchair is from The Charles Faudree Collection and was inspired by a fabric lining I found in an antique French armoire. It harmonizes beautifully with the drapery fabric, "Francoise," also from the collection. *Above:* Pillows can offer more than comfort for tired backs. The addition of an opulent tasseled fringe is a custom detail that elevates a nice pillow to a design focal point.

Opposite: A green silk velvet checked sofa serves as an arresting backdrop for chintz, silk and needlepoint pillows.

Right: Drapes can be important both for what they do and don't do. Simple unlined draperies in a muted checked fabric allow light to filter into my entrance hall; they take up very little visual space and let important antiques stand out. Solid-colored upholstery on the bench provides a neutral backdrop for the lovely antique fabric covering the pillows.

"Pillows are a wonderfully effective way
to introduce more fabrics."

Bob and Penny Downing's sofa is a neutral platform for a display of pillows that exudes welcoming comfort. Above them, greenery in a pair of Mason's ironstone vases echoes the foliage patterns of the pillow fabrics.

Opposite: My goal for the interior design of the Kappa Alpha Theta sorority at the University of Oklahoma was to provide an atmosphere for college living that wasn't sterile or painfully utilitarian. Custom details were the key. I used plenty of appealing fabric combinations, accent pillows, cording, tassels and fringe to create an inviting retreat from the hectic pace of college life. *Above:* The details of a pillow can create a charming relationship between fabrics. The custom cording and toile fabric of a chair are incorporated as trim and a medallion motif for the blue-and-white checked pillow, producing a one-of-a-kind accessory.

Above: A formal window treatment in Jeffrey and Lisa Rowsey's dining room includes rich toile side panels embellished with deeply fringed swags and jabots in the same fabric. Lace café curtains allow light while providing privacy. *Opposite:* Different textures and prints are used to highlight three pillows on a sofa in Jeff and Sheryl Bashaw's living room. Printed linen, old needlepoint tapestry and cut velvet fabrics share the limelight in this artful composition.

Opposite: Curtains in Peggy Puls' living room introduce a silk stripped fabric that reinforces the color scheme. The swags of the Kingston valance, mounted at the ceiling, increase the apparent height of the window and add to the formal elegance of the room. *Above:* Many of my designs are present in this fabric concoction, which includes checks in different sizes, stripes, a print, needlepoint and an oriental rug. They harmonize to create a uniquely inviting room, offering a perfect illustration of my philosophy, "It's all about the mix, not the match."

Above: A chair demonstrates how a lovely fabric can heighten the importance of an antique. Soft blue upholstery draws attention to the old blue paint finish of the chair's acanthus-leaf carving. *Opposite:* Custom pillows with toile inserts are the center of attention on a sofa in Drew and Ginny Webb's home.

Opposite: A silver chalice of tulips, an antique ice bucket and crystal decanters presented on a lovely silver tray create a useful tablescape that also functions as a bar in Roger and Kelly Ganner's dining room. A nineteenth-century French butcher's table and painted French side chairs covered in "Biron" checked fabric from The Charles Faudree Collection for Vervain form the backbone of the charming setting. *Above:* Fabrics used in Roger and Kelly Ganner's dressing room are as lavish and elegant as those used elsewhere in the home. Both antique and softly colored fabrics are used to create this personal haven.

Above: A splash of purple provided by a cut velvet throw accentuates a pastel bedroom haven in Jeffrey and Lisa Rowsey's home.

Opposite: "Mirabeau" fabric from The Charles Faudree Collection is used for the headboard in a pastel bedroom retreat in David and Cindy Foster's home. A touch of beading adds interest to a plain pillow.

Opposite:. A single fabric can provide the punctuation mark for a pretty room. An antique French toile fabric on a pillow with pom-pom fringe adds the finishing touch to a serene bedroom setting. *Above:* A combination of patterns and textures—and even a rhinestone or two—are the center of attention on the bed.

Above: A variety of textures—wool, silk, faux fur and antique needlepoint—enriches the subtle bed coverings, but nothing contributes more warmth and serenity to my bedroom retreat than my three Cavalier spaniels. *Opposite top:* Using an uncomplicated color scheme in shades of brown for the bed linens in my bedroom creates an understated environment for antique treasures.

*"It's about the mix
and not the match even
with Cavaliers."*

Opposite: An adroit use of formal materials to create an "unmade bed look" reveals layers of opulent fabrics that are simultaneously stately and inviting. The signature pillow was custom monogrammed for clients Frank and Gayle Eby.

Above: The bed pillows are lovely in their own right, but the addition of custom braiding to the printed linen pillows bestows a unique finishing touch.

Above: Fringed vertically striped taffeta drapery panels that are raised to ceiling height and extended to a slight break on the floor contribute a sumptuous feel to an elegant room in Frank and Leigh Ann Fore's home. Finishing the curtain rods with gold-painted rings adds luxurious detail. *Opposite:* A simple bed in Peggy Puls' home gets a royal treatment with a sumptuous bed hanging. The lavish use of fabric with contrasting fabric lining is enriched with fringe, rosettes and elaborate tassel tiebacks.

Opposite: A solid-colored wall and headboard provide a backdrop for the contrasting toiles used for the bed cover and curtains and the checked fabric of the bed skirt and valance trim. *Above:* A luxuriously fringed swag festoons matching floral linen drapes, adding to the garden-bower charm of this bedroom.

Above: The wildflowers and wildlife depicted in embroidered and appliquéd pillows produce a charming centerpiece for a secluded cabin's sofa. *Opposite:* The woodsy locale of Tom and Mickey Harris's cabin inspired the fanciful animal theme of the layered pillows on the living room sofa. Similarly, the boat painting, the shell box and even the pale, watery color scheme mirror the room's lakeside view.

Opposite: The velvet headboard and taffeta bed skirt add rich textures to the charming faded linen spread in John and Terry Mabrey's quiet guest room retreat. *Above:* "Hamlet's Toile," from The Charles Faudree Collection in an unusual lilac shade, adds interest to the European sham.

LIGHTING

When you think about decorating details, lighting probably isn't the first thing that comes to mind, but it is so very important. As a general rule, I'm not a big fan of track lighting or too many can lights. It's all too easy to turn a room into high noon, and the effect is harsh.

I prefer soft lamp lighting, and the older I get, the softer it gets. Soft lighting is far more flattering to rooms and to people, regardless of their age. Reading lamps need to be bright, but other lamps perform best with 40- or 60-watt bulbs. Overhead lighting can be attractive, too, as long as it has a dimmer switch.

Striking and unusual chandeliers are wonderful in the dining room. They should hang 30 to 36 inches above the table. Use clear bulbs with crystal chandeliers; all others should have frosted bulbs.

For the ultimate in elegant lighting, nothing is lovelier than candlelight. Of all the chandeliers I've owned over the years, my absolute favorite is one that uses real candles. The glow from the candles creates a festive atmosphere for a dinner party that is well worth a little extra trouble.

✳ ✳ ✳

Votives are a much simpler way to bring the warmth of candle-light to the table. Candelabras are an equally good option, as long as they have enough height so as not to obstruct conversation. And don't be concerned about making a choice between using a cande-labra or votives. This is one of those instances where my old credo "too much is not enough" applies. Why not just use both?

Candlelight can be used to cheer up other rooms, as well. Votives can be used anywhere. Included in a tablescape, they literally high-light other accessories. In guest baths, scented candles fall in the same category as linen hand towels and French soap: they suggest thoughtfulness and concern for visitors beyond the ordinary.

Wall sconces offer a special opportunity, simply because they are so seldom lighted. Lighting them highlights their beauty and adds warmth, gaiety, and the pleasure of the unexpected. I have a pair of toile sconces I bought in England long ago that have been traveling around with me for years. In my new home they occupy an impor-tant location over my living room mantel. I always light them for company, along with a pair of candlesticks I've added for even more inviting light.

Which brings me to my final thought: all those wonderful can-dles can't spread their cozy warmth if left unlighted. Lighting every single one might be excessive, but always light the wick at least once, so the candles show that they can be, and are, part of your cheerful life.

Opening overleaf: Lighting can be the focal point of a design. A wonderful hanging lantern and a sparkling pair of candelabras draped with glass beads dominate this hallway setting. *Previous page:* A pair of antique Staffordshire figures used for a custom lamp joins other pieces as part of a Staffordshire collection highlighting the desktop. *Above:* Tailoring details add distinction to the shade of a candlestick lamp. Bias banding and a circle inset are in the same stripe used for the shade.

Opposite: Restrained candlestick lamps are suitable companions for the august personage depicted in the oil painting above the antique chest in Susie Collins' home. *Above:* Pewter candlesticks modernized to become lamps wear custom shades made of "Le Luke" fabric from The Charles Faudree Collection.

Above: Even a small shade can benefit from two fabrics. A toile medallion centered on a blue-and-white-checked fabric creates an arresting look. *Opposite:* At their best, lamps become a part of the decorating scheme as well as illuminating it. The horn candlesticks I used for a pair of custom lamps are restatements of the horned animals heads mounted on the walls of my country home.

Opposite: A chandelier, candelabra and lamps combine to create a variety of interesting lighting for the dining room of the Mabrey home. *Above:* The festive atmosphere created by the use of real candles in a dining room chandelier elevates any dinner to special occasion status.

Above: The glow from a small pair of lamps adds to the warmth of a painted chest.

Opposite: Fine dressmaker details are evident in the pleated custom silk shades complementing an exceptional pair of antique candlesticks.

Opposite: Because of the scale of the antique Staffordshire figure used for its base, a lamp becomes the dominant piece of the tablescape. *Above:* The soft colors of the custom lamp duplicate the pastel fabrics used to create a pretty bedroom for two.

"For the ultimate in elegant lighting, nothing is lovelier than candlelight."

Above: Mirror-backed sconces flank a French gilt mirror to create a formal wallscape.

Opposite: Lighting in Mark Shires' bath has a rustic masculine appeal. Arresting metal candle sconces flanking the mirror are left without shades so that the unique pieces stand out.

Opposite: The old-world charm of candlelight as well as lamplight in Roger and Kelly Ganner's master bedroom enhances antique furnishings, including a wonderful Louis XV commode and antique wood panels hanging above the bed. *Above:* The decorative impact of any lighting source is limited only by imagination. An antique French crock, serving as the base of a lamp in a kitchen nook, adds one-of-a-kind appeal.

Above: An antique Staffordshire base depicting a trio of young maidens forms an appealing lamp base for milady's dresser. *Opposite:* A diminutive dressing table setting is perfectly matched with a mini chandelier and a single lamp. Fabric on the dressing stool is "François" from The Charles Faudree Collection.

Opposite: The antique metal figure makes a handsome custom lamp for my bedroom, but the addition of a custom shade with tassel trim makes it exceptional. *Above:* The pair of antique black candlesticks with custom toile-and-check shades becomes an important part of the tablescape.

Above: Elongated custom shield lampshades accentuate the height of their dramatic lamps.

Opposite: Contemporary lamps and custom shades add a strong architectural component to the top of a chest in Larry and Carol Bump's home.

* Resources *

CALIFORNIA

ANN DENNIS
2915 Red Hill Avenue, Suite B106
Costa Mesa, CA 92626
714-708-2555

HOLLYHOCK
927 North La Cienega Boulevard
Los Angeles, CA 90069
310-777-0100

TERRA COTTA
11920 San Vicente Boulevard
Los Angeles, CA 90046
310-826-7878

VILLA MELROSE
6061 West 3rd Street
Los Angeles, CA 90036
323-934-8130

JEFFRIES, LTD
852 Production Place
Newport Beach, CA 92663
949-642-4154

TOM STANSBURY ANTIQUES
466 Old Newport Boulevard
Newport Beach, CA 92663
949-642-1272

LIEF
646 North Almont Drive
West Hollywood, CA 90069
310-492-0033

COLORADO

GORSUCH, LTD
138 Beaver Creek Plaza
Avon, CO 81620
970-949-0786

GORSUCH. LTD
263 East Gore Creek Drive
Vail, CO 81657
970-476-2294

THE SHAGGY RAM
210 Edwards Village Boulevard #A-209
Edwards, CO 81632
970-926-7377

NEW YORK

JOHN DERIAN
6 East Second Street
New York City, NY 10003
212-677-3917

PIERRE DEUX
D&D Building
979 Third Avenue, Suite 134
New York City, NY 10022
212-644-4891

JOHN ROSSELLI
523 East 73rd Street
New York City, NY 10021
212-772-2137

ROYAL ANTIQUES
60 East 11th Street, Suite 1
New York City, NY 10003
212-533-6390

TREILLAGE, LTD
418 East 75th Street
New York City, NY 10021
212-535-2288

NORTH CAROLINA

VILLAGE ANTIQUES
755 Biltmore Avenue
Asheville, NC 28803
828-252-5090

DOVETAIL ANTIQUES
252 Highway 107 South
Cashiers, NC 28717
828-743-1800

FRANCIE HARGROVE
25 Burn Street
Cashiers, NC 28717
478-756-8088

RUSTICKS
32 Canoe Point
Cashiers, NC 28717
828-743-3172

RYAN & COMPANY
551 Highway 107 South
Cashiers, NC 28717
828-743-6767

VIVIANNE METZGER ANTIQUES
31 Canoe Point
Cashiers, NC 28717
828-743-0642

NEAL JOHNSON, LTD
601 South Cedar Street, Suite 205B
Charlotte, NC 28202
704-377-1099

ACORN'S BOUTIQUE
465 Main Street
Highlands, NC 28741
828-787-1877

C K SWAN & HARLEE GALLERY
233 North 4th Street
Highlands, NC 28741
828-526-2083

A COUNTRY HOME
5162 Cashiers Road
Highlands, NC 28741
828-526-9038

THOMAS HOKE ANTIQUES
WAREHOUSE
125 Lane Parkway
Salisbury, NC 28146
704-467-3456

OKLAHOMA

BEBE'S
6480 Avondale Drive
Oklahoma City, OK 73116
405-843-8431

COVINGTON ANTIQUES
7100 North Western Avenue
Oklahoma City, OK 73116
405-842-3030

THE ANTIQUARY
1325 East 15th Street, Suite 102
Tulsa, OK 74120
918-582-2897

ANTIQUE WAREHOUSE, DALE
GILLMAN
2406 East 12th Street
Tulsa, OK 74104
918-592-2900

EMBELLISHMENTS
1345 East 15th Street
Tulsa, OK 74120
918-585-8688

POLO LODGE ANTIQUES
8250 East 41st Street
Tulsa, OK 74145
918-622-3227

ROYCE MEYERS ART, LTD
1706 South Boston Avenue
Tulsa, OK 74119
918-582-0288

T. A. LORTON
1343 East 15th Street
Tulsa, OK 74120
918-743-1600

TONI'S FLOWERS
3549 South Harvard Avenue
Tulsa, OK 74135
918-742-9027

TENNESSEE
CATHERINE HARRIS
2215 Merchants Row, Suite 1
Germantown, TN 38138
901-753-0999

FRENCH COUNTRY IMPORTS
6225 Poplar Pike
Memphis, TN 38119
901-682-2000

JIMMY GRAHAM INTERIORS
3092 Poplar Avenue, Suite 17
Memphis, TN 38111
901-323-2322

MARKET CENTRAL
2215 Central Avenue
Memphis, TN 38104
901-276-3809

THE PALLADIO MARKET
2169 Central Avenue
Memphis, TN 38104
901-276-3808

TEXAS
COUNTRY FRENCH ANTIQUES
1428 Slocum Street
Dallas, TX 75207
215-747-4700

THE GATHERING GALLERIES
955 Slocum Street
Dallas, TX 75207
214-741-4888

INESSA STEWART'S ANTIQUES
5201 West Lovers Lane
Dallas, Texas 75209
214-366-2660

1643 Dragon Street
Dallas, TX 75207
214-742-5800

JOSEPH MINTON ANTIQUES
1410 Slocum Street
Dallas, TX 75207
214-744-3111

THE MEWS
1708 Market Center Boulevard
Dallas, TX 75207
214-748-9070

NICK BROCK ANTIQUES
2909 North Henderson Avenue
Dallas, TX 75206
214-828-0624

PIERRE DEUX
1525 Hi Line Drive
Dallas, TX 75207
214-749-7775

UNCOMMON MARKET
100 Riveredge Drive
Dallas, TX 75207
214-871-2775

THE WHIMSEY SHOP
1444 Oak Lawn Avenue, Suite 215
Dallas, TX 75207
214-745-1800

CHATEAU DOMINGUE
3615-B West Alabama Street
Houston, TX 77027
713-961-3444

GRAY DOOR
3465 West Alabama, Suite A
Houston, TX 77027
713-521-9085

JOYCE HORN ANTIQUES, LTD
1022 Wirt Road, Suite 326
Houston, TX 77055
713-688-0507

KAY O'TOOLE ANTIQUES &
ECCENTRICITIES
1921 Westheimer Road
Houston, TX 77098
713-523-1921

NEAL AND COMPANY ANTIQUES
4502 Greenbriar Street
Houston, TX 77005
713-942-9800

WATKINS CULVER ANTIQUES
2308 Bissonnet Street
Houston, TX 77005
713-529-0597

WHITE & DAY ANTIQUES
6711 FM 1960 Road West
Houston, TX 77069
281-444-3836

Acknowledgments

I've said many times that the details of decorating give a home its soul. They are the frosting on the cake. In the same way the many friends I work with and my loyal clients—also my good friends—are the frosting on my professional career. Their warmth and affection add the special details that complete my life and enrich my soul. I thank all of them for making this book a reality. Sincere thanks:

For my wonderful clients, who allowed me to create beautiful rooms and graciously consented to let them to be photographed: Steve and Gayle Allen, Jeff and Sheryl Bashaw, Larry and Carol Bump, Susie Collins, Bob and Penny Downing, Frank and Gayle Eby, Frank and Leigh Ann Fore, Roger and Kelly Ganner, Tom and Mickey Harris, John and Terry Mabrey, Peggy Puls, Jeffrey and Lisa Rowsey Mark and Cassie Shires, the women of Alpha Omicron Chapter of Kappa Alpha Theta at The University of Oklahoma and Drew and Ginny Webb.

For Jenifer Jordan, for her photography and for her wonderful eye. For her talent, and high standard of excellence. Thanks for the friendship and all the fun we had together—and there's more fun to come.

For Francesanne—what a joy to work with—for taking my ramblings and half-sentences and making them coherent. Thanks for a great job and wonderful friendship.

For everyone in my shop: Megan, Darcie, Mary Dale, George, Bill and John. You kept things together while I was away photographing and working.

For Madge, my friend and editor. You have always kept me on the path for deadlines and talked me through my concerns. Thanks for you amazing ability to "wear so many different hats" to make things work.

For Toni Garner, for always arriving with the perfect flowers at a moment's notice.

Once again, I'm grateful for my sister and my partner, Francie Faudree Gillman and Bill Carpenter. Your stability, love and support are truly gifts to treasure.

Finally, a pat for Nicholas. Ruby and Lila. This book would not be complete without my beloved Cavaliers.